A Guide to
AMERICAN STATES

Arizona

THE GRAND CANYON STATE

www.av2books.com

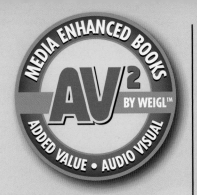

AV² provides enriched content that supplements and complements this book. Weigl's AV² books strive to create inspired learning and engage young minds in a total learning experience.

Your AV² Media Enhanced books come alive with...

Audio
Listen to sections of the book read aloud.

Key Words
Study vocabulary, and complete a matching word activity.

Go to **www.av2books.com**, and enter this book's unique code.

Video
Watch informative video clips.

Quizzes
Test your knowledge.

BOOK CODE

A 2 1 5 1 0 4

Embedded Weblinks
Gain additional information for research.

Slide Show
View images and captions, and prepare a presentation.

AV² by Weigl brings you media enhanced books that support active learning.

Try This!
Complete activities and hands-on experiments.

... and much, much more!

Published by AV² by Weigl
350 5th Avenue, 59th Floor
New York, NY 10118
Website: www.av2books.com   www.weigl.com

Library of Congress Cataloging-in-Publication Data

Craats, Rennay.
 Arizona / Rennay Craats.
    p. cm.
 Includes index.
 ISBN 978-1-61690-775-4 (hardcover : alk. paper) -- ISBN 978-1-61690-450-0 (online)
 1. Arizona--Juvenile literature. I. Title.
 F811.3.C73 2011
 979.1--dc22
                                    2011018314

Printed in the United States of America in North Mankato, Minnesota

052011
WEP180511

Project Coordinator Jordan McGill
Art Director Terry Paulhus

Photo Credits
Every reasonable effort has been made to trace ownership and to obtain permission to reprint copyright material. The publishers would be pleased to have any errors or omissions brought to their attention so that they may be corrected in subsequent printings.

Weigl acknowledges Getty Images as its primary image supplier for this title.

Contents

The Grand Canyon is Arizona's most popular tourist attraction.

Introduction

The Grand Canyon State was once considered to be little more than a barren desert, but vast **irrigation** systems have transformed the dry desert soil into successful farmland. The mild winters and dry summers have attracted so many people that Arizona is one of the country's fastest-growing states. Between 2000 and 2009 the population increased by nearly 30 percent.

While most of the people live in the southern part of the state, the northern half contains some of the most breathtaking scenery in the country. Arizona received its nickname from the Grand Canyon, a spectacular landform located in the northwestern part of the state. It took the Colorado River about 6 million years to carve out the

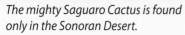
The mighty Saguaro Cactus is found only in the Sonoran Desert.

The Colorado River cuts through the Grand Canyon.

Grand Canyon. This immense **gorge** is 18 miles across at its widest point, more than 1 mile below the Earth's surface at its deepest, and 277 miles long. Within the canyon are impressive **mesas** and **buttes** formed by the action of water on the rocks. The layers of rock in the canyon reveal the history of Arizona. Different kinds of limestone, sandstone, and shale are stacked like pancakes in the Earth. Some of the fossils and deposits found in this area are hundreds of millions of years old. The canyon, and part of the plateau surrounding it, is preserved as Grand Canyon National Park. Nearly 5 million people view the canyon every year. They can explore by peering over the edge or taking a bus tour along the rim. Others rent mules and ride down into the canyon or hike down on their own. Visitors can also fly over the canyon in helicopters and airplanes. River rafters brave the Colorado River to observe the Grand Canyon from within.

Where Is Arizona?

Arizona is a large state located in the southwestern United States. The Colorado River defines most of the western border, but otherwise the boundary lines are straight. Utah lies to the north, New Mexico to the east, and Nevada and California to the west. Across an international boundary to the south is the Mexican state of Sonora. Arizona has six interstate highways within the state. However, parts of the north, especially in the Grand Canyon region, are somewhat more **isolated** than the south.

Arizona is part of the Four Corners, which is the only place in the United States where the boundaries of four states meet.

Most travelers who arrive in Arizona by air fly into either Phoenix or Tucson. Phoenix's airport, Sky Harbor International, carries more passengers than any other airport in the state and is one of the world's busiest in numbers of takeoffs and landings. It serves as a hub for flights to a number of other cities within Arizona.

Temperatures in Phoenix can easily reach 110° Fahrenheit in the summer, but humidity is low and almost every building and vehicle is air conditioned. In the winter, while much of the nation is shivering with cold, Arizonans bask in warmth. This makes the state an ideal winter getaway. A large number of retired people, often called "snowbirds," drive south and spend their winters in Arizona. The state's permanent residents include many retirees as well, but people of all ages have flocked to the state for the favorable climate and career opportunities.

Many people come to Arizona to enjoy its numerous golf courses.

Mapping Arizona

Arizona is bordered by Utah on the north, Mexico to the south, New Mexico to the east, and California and Nevada to the west. The western border is defined by the Colorado River. The majority of the state's population lives in its largest cities, Phoenix and Tucson.

Sites and Symbols

STATE SEAL
Arizona

STATE BIRD
Cactus Wren

STATE GEMSTONE
Turquoise

STATE FLAG
Arizona

STATE FOSSIL
Petrified Wood

STATE TREE
Palo Verde

Nickname The Grand Canyon State

Motto *Ditat Deus* (God Enriches)

Song "Arizona March Song," words by Margaret Rowe Clifford and music by Maurice Blumenthal

Entered the Union February 14, 1912, as the 48th state

Capital Phoenix

Population (2010 Census) 6,392,017 Ranked 16th State

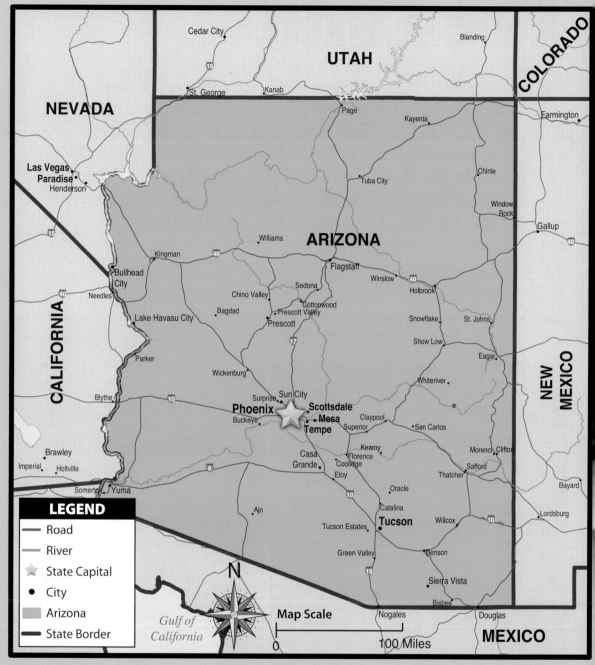

Cedar City

UTAH

Blanding

St. George Kanab

NEVADA

Page

Kayenta

Farmington

Las Vegas
Paradise
Henderson

Chinle

Tuba City

Window
Rock

Gallup

Williams

ARIZONA

Kingman

Flagstaff

Winslow

Holbrook

Bullhead
City

Needles

Chino Valley

Sedona

Snowflake

St. Johns

Cottonwood

Bagdad

Prescott Valley

Show Low

Lake Havasu City

Prescott

Eagar

CALIFORNIA

Parker

Whiteriver

Blythe

Wickenburg

Sun City

Surprise

Scottsdale

Phoenix

Mesa

Claypool

Buckeye

Tempe

Superior

San Carlos

Morenci Clifton

Kearny

Florence

NEW MEXICO

Safford

Brawley

Casa
Grande

Coolidge

Thatcher

Imperial Holtville

Eloy

Bayard

Oracle

Somerton Yuma

Catalina

Lordsburg

Ajo

Tucson Estates

Willcox

Tucson

Green Valley

Benson

Gulf of
California

Sierra Vista

Bisbee

Nogales

Douglas

MEXICO

LEGEND

— Road
— River
⭐ State Capital
● City
▢ Arizona
— State Border

N

Map Scale

0   100 Miles

STATE CAPITAL

Phoenix, with a population of 1.6 million, is Arizona's capital and largest city.

In 2010, the city's average high summer temperature was 105°F.

United States

Arizona

Hawai'i Alaska

The Land

Although most of Arizona's people live in desert areas, more than half of the state is mountains and plateaus. The main land regions are the Colorado Plateau and the Basin and Range region, with a transition zone between them. The Colorado Plateau is a dry, flat region that covers northern Arizona. It ends with the steep rock wall of the Mogollon Rim. The transition zone is a strip of land south of the Colorado Plateau that includes several mountain ranges. The Basin and Range region, which covers most of the south and some of the west of Arizona, is very dry. It includes the Sonoran Desert, which extends into Mexico.

THE GRAND CANYON

Located in the western part of the Colorado Plateau, the Grand Canyon is 277 miles long.

SONORAN DESERT

The cactus-filled Sonoran Desert covers the southern third of Arizona.

HUMPREYS PEAK

The highest point in the state is Humphreys Peak. It rises 12,633 feet above sea level.

OAK CREEK CANYON

Not all of Arizona is dry. Oak Creek Canyon has natural swimming holes.

The Colorado River is the lowest point in the state, at 70 feet above sea level.

Monument Valley lies entirely within the Navajo reservation on the Utah-Arizona border.

The Painted Desert, named for its colorful rock formations, runs for more than 160 miles along the Little Colorado River.

Most Arizonans endure blistering temperatures in the summer months.

Climate

Arizona's largest city, Phoenix, is located in the Sonoran Desert. Phoenix endures more than 90 days a year when the mercury soars above 100° F. Before the invention of air conditioning, it was a difficult place for people to live. While minimum temperatures in the desert may not dip below freezing in a typical year, winter temperatures in the mountains can fall to 0° F. Vast desert regions receive less than 10 inches of rain per year, but the state's northern and eastern mountain ranges get more than 25 inches. Snow is common in the mountains.

Average July Temperatures Across Arizona

Arizona is known for its hot summers, but in some parts of the state the temperatures are mild. Why do you think Flagstaff's July temperatures are so much lower than those in Phoenix?

Degrees Fahrenheit

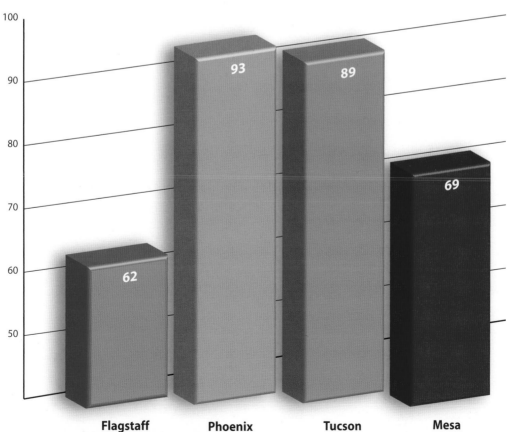

Flagstaff	Phoenix	Tucson	Mesa
62	93	89	69

Natural Resources

Arizona's first European settlers were lured to the state by its wealth of minerals. Today natural resources remain important to the state's economy. Arizona is rich in copper, supplying about two-thirds of the nation's total production. There are open-pit and underground copper mines in many parts of the state. Sand and gravel are mined in Arizona and are used in construction. Other key minerals in the state include gold, molybdenum, silver, gypsum, and gemstones.

The Morenci Copper Mine is one of the largest open-pit mines in the world.

Water is a precious resource in Arizona. The first system of irrigation canals was dug by the prehistoric Hohokam people. Some of these canals are still used to bring water to crops. Water-management projects on a larger scale have been built in recent times. Many dams, such as the giant Hoover Dam on the Nevada border, have been built to create reservoirs for water storage and to produce **hydroelectricity**.

The Hoover Dam was built in the 1930s. Its construction formed Lake Mead, one of the largest artificial lakes in the world.

Molybdenum mined in Arizona is used to harden steel.

In the Superstition Mountains east of Phoenix, prospectors still search for the Lost Dutchman Gold Mine. It is said that a miner named Jacob Waltz took the secret of its location to his grave in 1891.

Arizona's irrigated cropland is some of the most valuable farmland in the United States.

Visitors to Arizona can take tours of old copper mines.

The area between the Colorado Plateau and the lower Basin and Range region is often called "the copper belt" because it is rich with deposits of copper-bearing minerals.

Plants

Many types of cacti grow in Arizona. The largest is the majestic saguaro, which can grow to a height of 50 feet and live for as long as 200 years. The white blossom of this cactus is the state flower. Prickly pear, barrel, and organ-pipe cacti also grow in Arizona. Cacti survive in the desert climate because they are able to store water in their stems and roots. Other desert plants, including creosote and sagebrush, also store moisture well.

Not all of Arizona is desert. Almost one-quarter of the state is forested. The trees grow mostly at higher elevations. One of the most common trees in Arizona is the ponderosa pine. Aspen, cottonwood, blue spruce, and walnut trees are also found in the state.

POPPIES

Poppies are common wildflowers in southern Arizona

SAGUARO CACTUS

The large saguaro cactus can grow to be 30 feet tall or more.

MESQUITE TREE

The mesquite tree is one of the state's most common desert trees.

JOSHUA TREE

The largest member of the yucca family is the Joshua tree. It is dominant in the western deserts.

More than 400 edible plants grow in the Sonoran Desert.

The teddy bear cholla cactus looks soft and fuzzy from a distance, but its spines are barbed and sharp.

The Gila Woodpecker and the Gilded Flicker make homes inside the Saguaro Cactus by carving out holes in the trunk.

The palo verde tree's name is Spanish for "green stick."

Animals

It takes hardy animals to live in some of the harsh areas of Arizona. Many different kinds of lizards, including the poisonous Gila monster, roam the state. Scorpions and tarantulas inhabit the hotter areas. Rattlesnakes and coral snakes may be found slithering along the desert floor. Desert mule deer graze on cactus fruit in the winter and look for higher scrub forests for food in the summer.

In Arizona's grasslands, herds of pronghorn antelope share pastures with domestic cattle and sheep. White-tailed deer, elks, and mountain lions are found in the forests. Foxes, badgers, and wild piglike animals called javelinas all live on Arizona's varied land. In the sky, eagles soar near the mountains and vultures circle the desert floor. Roadrunners and wild turkeys are also found in the state.

DESERT TORTOISE

The desert tortoise has forelimbs that are adapted for digging through desert sand to find shelter from heat and predators.

MULE DEER

The mule deer, which has large ears like a mule, lives throughout the state. These deer are known for their black-tipped tails.

WESTERN DIAMONDBACK RATTLESNAKE

Arizona is home to 13 different types of rattlesnakes, more than any other state. The Western Diamondback is the largest rattlesnake native to Arizona. It can grow to more than seven feet long.

MOUNTAIN LION

Mountain lions are the largest wild cats in the United States. They can be found throughout the state, but these solitary animals avoid people and are rarely seen in the wild.

The javelina eats grasses, fruits, and seeds, but its favorite food is the prickly pear cactus.

Arizona's collared lizards run on their hind legs when they are alarmed.

Tourism

The Grand Canyon is Arizona's most popular tourist destination. People can also visit the buttes and mesas of Monument Valley and the Meteor Crater, a pit nearly a mile across and 550 feet deep where a meteorite struck the Earth about 50,000 years ago. Arizona is also home to many American Indian reservations. Visitors go to the reservations to see traditional ceremonies, gamble at casinos, and to buy American Indian arts and crafts.

Arizona's Wild West heritage is preserved in Tombstone, where the fabled gunfight at the O.K. Corral was fought. Restored saloons and reenactments give visitors a sense of the unruly lifestyles of Arizona frontier towns.

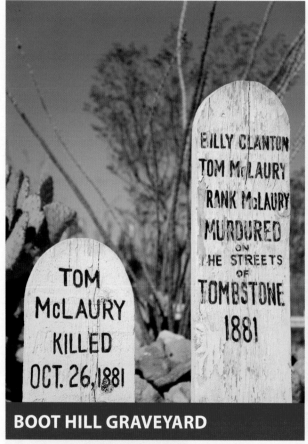

BOOT HILL GRAVEYARD

The Boot Hill Graveyard in Tombstone gives visitors a chilling reminder of what a dangerous place the Old West could be.

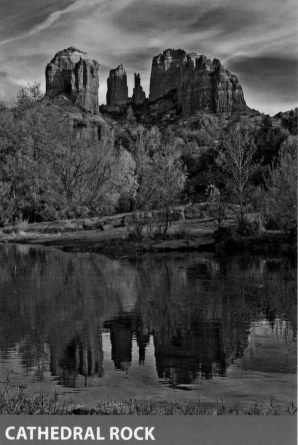

CATHEDRAL ROCK

Iron oxide, or rust, gives Cathedral Rock in Sedona its reddish coloration.

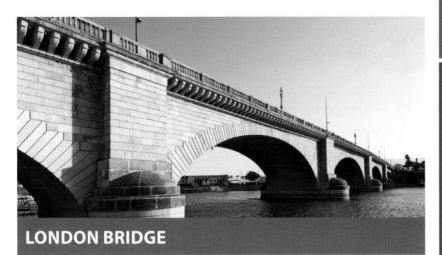

LONDON BRIDGE

Lake Havasu City's London Bridge, which was the inspiration for the song "London Bridge Is Falling Down," spanned the Thames River in England before being sold to an American in the late 1960s. It was shipped to Arizona and reassembled in the Mojave Desert.

PETRIFIED FOREST

In the **Petrified** Forest, visitors can view giant logs that turned to a rocklike material over millions of years.

The mining town of Tombstone survived the decline in the silver-mining industry and earned the nickname "Town Too Tough to Die."

The Phoenix Zoo, which opened in 1962, is one of the largest private non-profit zoos in the United States. It is home to more than 1,300 animals.

Super Bowl XLII brought many visitors to Arizona. The game, which took place in February 2008, was played at the University of Phoenix stadium in Glendale. The New York Giants defeated the New England Patriots by a score of 17–14.

Industry

Arizona has more than 25 million acres of farmland, but very little of this land is used to grow crops. Most of the land is used to raise livestock, and cattle sales make up the largest source of income for farmers and ranchers annually. Arizona has more than 1 million head of cattle, and the state produces more than 380 million pounds of beef every year.

Industries in Arizona
Value of Goods and Services in Millions of Dollars

Arizona has many different kinds of industries. The state manufactures many different kinds of products. Service industries, which provide a service for someone else, are also very important. Restaurant workers and computer repair people are both considered part of the service industry. Why might service industries contribute so much to the state's economy?

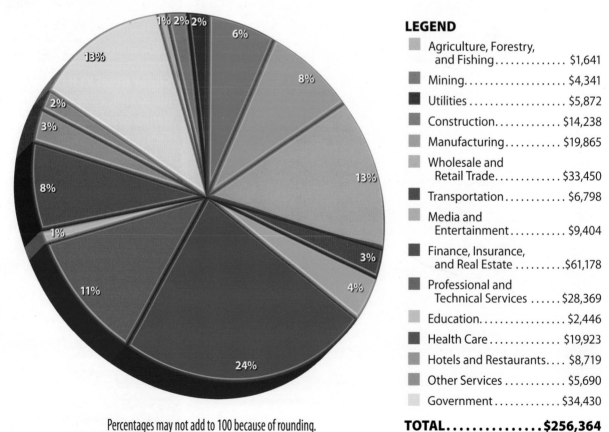

Percentages may not add to 100 because of rounding.

LEGEND

Industry	Value
Agriculture, Forestry, and Fishing	$1,641
Mining	$4,341
Utilities	$5,872
Construction	$14,238
Manufacturing	$19,865
Wholesale and Retail Trade	$33,450
Transportation	$6,798
Media and Entertainment	$9,404
Finance, Insurance, and Real Estate	$61,178
Professional and Technical Services	$28,369
Education	$2,446
Health Care	$19,923
Hotels and Restaurants	$8,719
Other Services	$5,690
Government	$34,430
TOTAL	**$256,364**

Arizona is known for its "Five Cs": copper, citrus, cattle, climate, and cotton. Cotton is one of Arizona's most important crops. The warm, sunny climate also makes Arizona an important fruit and vegetable producer, especially during the winter, when farms in northern states are shut down. Miles of lemon, orange, and grapefruit groves line the desert.

Arizona's climate is ideal for growing many kinds of crops, including oranges.

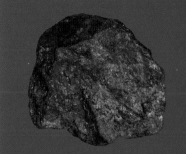

Located in southeast Arizona, the Morenci Mine is the largest copper mine in the country.

In addition to cotton and citrus fruits, Arizona farmers grow lettuce, melons, spinach, and alfalfa.

Mining is an important industry in Arizona. In addition to copper, molybdenum, silver, gemstones, sand, and gravel are all mined in the state.

The city of Yuma is known as the "Winter Lettuce Capital of the World" and celebrates with a festival every year.

Goods and Services

Most of Arizona's manufacturing plants are located in the Phoenix and Tucson areas. Electronics goods are very important to this sector of the economy. Some manufacturers produce space vehicles and guided missiles for the government. Others produce aeronautical products and parts. With the growth of the computer industry, Arizona manufacturers are making a variety of semiconductors and other electronics components. Metal processing is also an important industry.

Arizona is a great place to go trail riding. Many places offer horseback riding lessons.

In addition to being Arizona's top tourist attraction, the Grand Canyon is one of the most popular vacation sites in all of the United States.

The Arizona Republic, printed in Phoenix, has more readers than any other newspaper in Arizona. Other popular papers include *The Tucson Citizen* and *The Arizona Daily Star*, which is also printed in Tucson. Arizonans trumpet the attractions of their state in a magazine called *Arizona Highways*, which since 1925 has circulated widely throughout the United States. All of these publications are available online.

Many Arizonans work in service occupations. These are workers who do something for someone else. Many service providers support the state's strong tourism industry. Attractions such as the Grand Canyon and the state's many **dude ranches** contribute to the success of the tourism industry.

American Indians

The presence of American Indian culture is felt more strongly in Arizona than in almost any other state. There is evidence that people have lived in what is now Arizona for more than 12,000 years. American Indian cultures of recent times developed out of the cultures of earlier settlers. One of first groups to live in what is now Arizona, the Ancestral Puebloan people, built dwellings into the sides of cliffs that can still be seen today. In the Gila and Salt River valleys, the Hohokam dug irrigation ditches to water the crops they planted in the desert fields. The Mogollon lived in the east, where they made the region's first pottery. The Sinagua lived in the northwest. The Navajo and the Apaches began moving into the area from the north in about 1250. The Navajo grew crops and raised sheep in the northeast. The Apaches hunted game in the southern mountains.

Homes built by the Sinagua can be seen at Montezuma Castle National Monument, near Camp Verde.

As settlers from farther east in the United States moved into Arizona in the 1800s, many American Indians were forced from their land. In 1864, U.S. Army troops, led by Christopher "Kit" Carson, chased the Navajo out of their canyon homes and burned their crops. About 8,000 Navajo were captured and forced to make their way to eastern New Mexico on foot. Today, this 300-mile trek is known as the Long Walk. Finally, a new **treaty** was signed in 1868, and the surviving Navajo were allowed to go back to a reservation in Arizona.

Kit Carson led U.S. troops that fought the Navajo in the 1860s.

Apache groups fought against the United States for many years. Most were never defeated, but the Apache leader Cochise decided to stop fighting and surrendered in 1871.

Casa Grande, a four-story structure between Phoenix and Tucson, was built by the Hohokam. The ruins can be viewed at Casa Grande Ruins National Monument.

The Hopi of today are believed to be related to the Ancestral Puebloan people. The Pima and the Tohono O'odham are thought to have descended from the Hohokam.

Explorers and Missionaries

By the 1520s the Spanish had conquered Mexico. Soon afterward they heard rumors of fabulous riches to the north. In 1539, Marcos de Niza led an **expedition** into Arizona in search of the legendary Seven Cities of Cíbola, which were said to have streets of gold. The following year Francisco Vázquez de Coronado traveled through Arizona, also in search of treasure. But the bricks he found in the American Indian villages were **adobe**, not gold. Coronado's men were the first Europeans to behold the Grand Canyon.

In 1629, Spanish missionaries arrived in Arizona at the Hopi mesas. They hoped to convert the American Indians to Christianity. The Indians were forbidden to practice their own religion. In 1680, the Pueblo Indians in New Mexico rebelled against the Spanish and drove them out of the area. The Hopi in Arizona followed suit. Missionaries had better luck in southern Arizona. A Spanish priest named Eusebio Kino was respectful to the Indians, teaching them new ways to farm and raise cattle and sheep. Kino set up 24 missions in Arizona and New Mexico.

The San Xavier del Bac Mission, which was founded by Eusebio Kino, is still used for church services.

Timeline of Settlement

Early Exploration

1539 Marcos de Niza leads an expedition into present-day Arizona in search of the legendary Seven Cities of Cíbola.

1540 Francisco Vázquez de Coronado and his men, looking for riches, are the first Europeans to sight the Grand Canyon.

Conflict with American Indians

1629 Spanish soldiers supervise the building of missions throughout present-day Arizona and New Mexico.

1680 The Pueblo people rebel in New Mexico and drive the missionaries out of the area.

1752 To protect themselves from attacks by American Indians, Spanish soldiers build a walled presidio, or fort, at Tubac.

Struggles for Independence

1821 After eleven years of war, Mexico wins independence from Spain. Present-day Arizona becomes part of Mexico.

1848 A huge portion of the Southwest, including almost all of present-day Arizona, is transferred from Mexico to the United States.

1853 Mexico agrees to sell the United States a strip of land, known as the Gadsden Purchase, that finalizes Arizona's southern border.

1846 The Mexican-American War begins between the United States and Mexico.

Statehood

1863 President Abraham Lincoln signs a bill creating the Territory of Arizona.

1912 Arizona becomes a state on February 14th, when President William Howard Taft approves the state constitution.

Early Settlers

I n 1752, the Spanish built a military post at Tubac in response to clashes with American Indians. This fort became Arizona's first European settlement. More military forts, including one at Tucson in 1776, were built to protect Spanish interests in the area. However, it was not long before the Spanish lost control of Arizona to Mexico.

Map of Settlements and Resources in Early Arizona

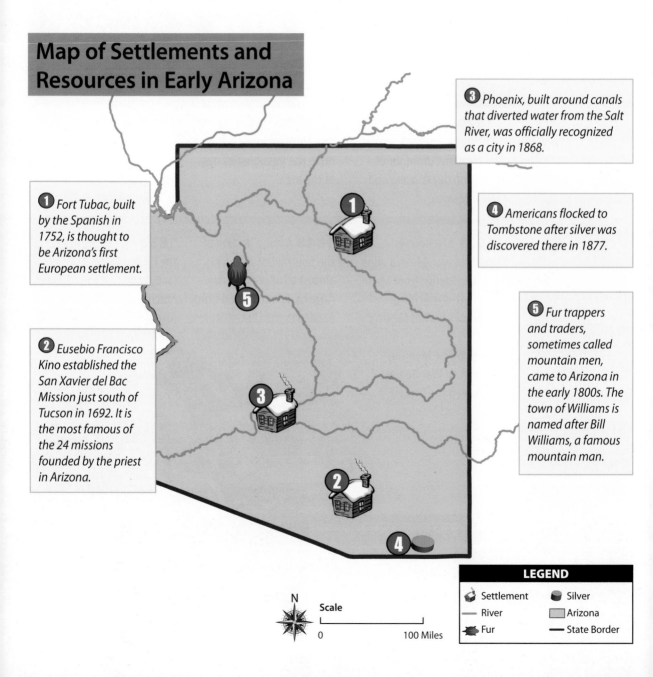

3 *Phoenix, built around canals that diverted water from the Salt River, was officially recognized as a city in 1868.*

1 *Fort Tubac, built by the Spanish in 1752, is thought to be Arizona's first European settlement.*

4 *Americans flocked to Tombstone after silver was discovered there in 1877.*

2 *Eusebio Francisco Kino established the San Xavier del Bac Mission just south of Tucson in 1692. It is the most famous of the 24 missions founded by the priest in Arizona.*

5 *Fur trappers and traders, sometimes called mountain men, came to Arizona in the early 1800s. The town of Williams is named after Bill Williams, a famous mountain man.*

N

Scale

0   100 Miles

LEGEND

Settlement		Silver	
River		Arizona	
Fur		State Border	

While Arizona was under Spanish and Mexican control, few people were interested in the region. Only a few American explorers, soldiers, trappers, and sheep drivers visited the area. In 1848, after a war with Mexico, the United States took over an immense tract of land in the Southwest, including most of Arizona. The signing of the Treaty of Guadalupe Hidalgo ended the war. The United States bought the rest of the land that became Arizona from Mexico in the Gadsden Purchase of 1853.

The Mexican-American War lasted from 1846 to 1848. The Battle of Palo Alto was the first major battle in the war.

I DIDN'T KNOW THAT!

The United States paid about $15 million to compensate Mexico for the territory it gave up after the Mexican-American War.

Eusebio Kino made several maps of Arizona. The maps were used for many years after his death.

Arizona's gold and silver rush during the mid-1800s and late 1800s attracted lawless fortune hunters to the area. Residents, including Wyatt and Virgil Earp, "Doc" Holliday, and the Clanton gang, became legendary gunfighters and lawmakers in Tombstone.

In 1768, Francisco Tomás Garcés began missionary work in Arizona. He traveled widely in the area before being killed during a Yuma uprising in 1781.

Notable People

Many notable Arizonans contributed to the development of their state and country. Environmentalist Edward Abbey lived in Oracle. William Rehnquist practiced law in Phoenix before becoming Chief Justice of the Supreme Court in 1986. A number of important politicians have made their home in Arizona. Two of these politicians, Barry Goldwater and John McCain, ran for president. Though both were defeated, they continued to make important contributions to politics after the elections.

GERONIMO
(1829–1909)

Apache leader Geronimo helped his people fight back after they were forced onto a reservation by the U.S. government in 1874. After years of suffering and several escape attempts, Geronimo fled from the reservation and hid in the mountains in Mexico. He led several attacks on settlements, but Geronimo eventually surrendered to the U.S. Army in 1886.

WYATT EARP
(1848–1929)

Law enforcement official Wyatt Earp is best-known for his participation in the gunfight at the O.K. Corral, which took place in Tombstone. The gunfight is one of the most well-known in history, and has been dramatized in many movies over the years, but it lasted only 30 seconds.

PERCIVAL LOWELL (1855–1916)

Born in Boston, astronomer Percival Lowell moved to Flagstaff as an adult and founded the Lowell Observatory. He is best-known for initiating the search that discovered Pluto. When Lowell died in 1916, he left money to the observatory to help keep its research going.

CÉSAR CHÁVEZ (1927–1993)

Hispanic American César Chávez was born in Yuma. During the Great Depression, a time of widespread economic hardship, Chávez's family was kicked off their farm for failing to pay taxes. In 1962, he founded the union that would later become the United Farm Workers. Through peaceful protests, Chávez won many improvements in the wages and working conditions of farm workers. He stood up for workers until his death in 1993.

SANDRA DAY O'CONNOR (1930–)

Texas-born Sandra Day O'Connor spent a large part of her childhood on her family's cattle ranch near Duncan. In 1981, O'Connor made history when she became the first woman appointed to the U.S. Supreme Court. She served as a Supreme Court justice until 2006.

I DIDN'T KNOW THAT!

Architect Frank Lloyd Wright (1867–1959) built his winter home and school in Scottsdale in 1937. Called Taliesin West, it is today the main campus of the Frank Lloyd Wright School of Architecture. It is open to the public for tours.

Sharlot Hall (1870–1943) was thrown from a horse at age 11, while her family was traveling from Kansas to the Arizona Territory. She began writing to distract herself from an injured spine, which would cause her pain for the rest of her life. Her work as a journalist and poet led to a job as the territorial historian. She restored the log building in Prescott that had been the territory's first **capitol** and governor's mansion. Today the mansion is known as the Sharlot Hall Museum.

Population

More than 280,000 American Indians live in Arizona. Only California has a larger American Indian population. A majority of Arizonans are of European **ancestry**. More than 30 percent claim Hispanic roots. The vast majority of these are Mexican Americans. African Americans make up about 4 percent of Arizona's total population, and Asian Americans make up about 2 percent.

Most of Arizona's population is concentrated in its large cities. Phoenix is home to 1.6 million residents. Other large cities include Tucson, Glendale, Mesa, Chandler, and Scottsdale.

Arizona Population 1950-2010

The population of Arizona has increased sharply in the past 60 years. What are the different factors that contribute to a state's population growth?

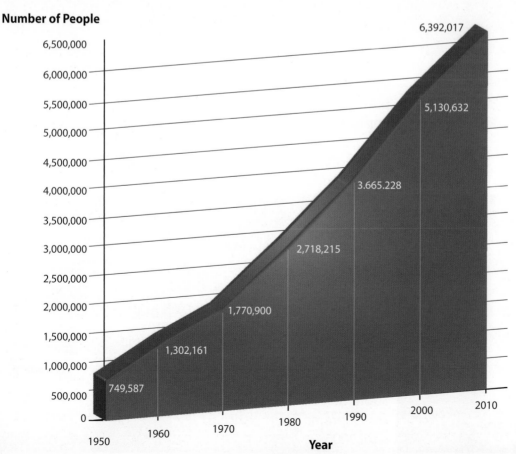

Number of People

Year	Population
1950	749,587
1960	1,302,161
1970	1,770,900
1980	2,718,215
1990	3,665,228
2000	5,130,632
2010	6,392,017

More American Indians live in Arizona than in most other U.S. states.

Children make up 26 percent of Arizona's population.

I DIDN'T KNOW THAT!

Arizona's largest county by population is Maricopa.

The invention of air conditioning in the 1950s caused a boom in Arizona's population.

The Hopi town of Oraibi, which dates back to about 1150, may be the oldest continuously inhabited settlement in the United States.

Politics and Government

Arizona holds many firsts in politics and government. In 1981, Sandra Day O'Connor became the first female justice appointed to the U.S. Supreme Court. In 1998, the state became the first in history to elect women to the top five executive offices.

The original Arizona State Capitol Building opened in 1901. Today it serves as a state historical museum.

The Arizona government is structured much like the federal government. It has executive, legislative, and judicial branches. The executive branch is led by the governor, who is elected to a four-year term. The governor appoints officials, sets the budget, and decides which state issues are most important. The legislature is composed of a Senate of 30 members and a House of Representatives of 60 members.

John McCain, a U.S. senator from Arizona since 1987, was the Republican nominee for president in 2008. He lost the election to Barack Obama.

Arizona's state song is called "Arizona March Song."

Here is an excerpt from the song:

Not alone for gold and silver
Is Arizona great.
But with graves of heroes sleeping,
All the land is consecrate!
O, come and live beside us
However far ye roam
Come and help us build up temples
And name those temples "home."

Sing the song that's in your hearts
Sing of the great Southwest,
Thank God, for Arizona
In splendid sunshine dressed.
For thy beauty and thy grandeur,
For thy regal robes so sheen
We hail thee Arizona
Our Goddess and our queen.

John McCain, who moved to Arizona in the early 1980s, has been elected to the U.S. Senate five times by the state's voters.

Cultural Groups

Hispanic culture thrives in the state of Arizona. The ancestors of some Hispanic Arizonans lived in the region long before Arizona became a part of the United States. Especially in southern Arizona, many people are **bilingual**, capable of speaking both Spanish and English. On September 16, festivals celebrate Mexican Independence Day. Throughout the state parties featuring **mariachi** bands and fireworks celebrate Mexico's successful fight for independence from Spain.

As a Southwestern state, Arizona embraces cowboy culture. Many of the first cowboys were Mexican, and some of the cowboy terms used today have Mexican origins. Vaquero became "buckaroo" in English, *la reata* became "**lariat**," and *chaparreras* were leather leggings worn by cowboys that became known as "chaps." Tucson celebrates its Mexican cowboy culture during La Fiesta de los Vaqueros.

Because of the state's large Hispanic population, many people in Arizona celebrate Mexican Independence Day on September 16th.

The Roy Track Memorial Mesa Powwow is held in Mesa every fall. Local tribes celebrate with traditional music, food, and dancing.

Of all the states, Arizona has the most land set aside for Indian reservations.

Spanish and Mexican influences in Arizona can be seen in the style of buildings and in place names.

The Navajo Reservation, which is located in northeastern Arizona and parts of Utah and New Mexico, is about the size of West Virginia.

The Arizona Matsuri, held in Phoenix every February, celebrates Japanese culture with music, crafts, food, and art.

Arizona's Western culture shows in its choice of official state neckwear. The bolo tie, invented in Arizona, was and still is a favorite among cowboys.

During the 1800s many people from Europe arrived in Arizona to work in copper mines. Some African Americans moved to Arizona to work on ranches. In the 1850s, many Chinese people came to the state to build railroads and work in mines. Other people of Asian descent have since moved to Arizona, enriching the state with their cultures and traditions. Japanese culture is celebrated every year in Phoenix with the Matsuri festival. During this celebration, people can enjoy traditional Japanese foods and watch martial arts performances.

Every September the Navajo celebrate their traditions at the Navajo Nation Fair in Window Rock, the capital of the Navajo Reservation. It is said to be the biggest American Indian fair in the world. The fair features rodeos, parades, and exhibits of Navajo artwork and crafts.

Arts and Entertainment

Arizona's picturesque landscape has served as inspiration to many talented artists. The landscape painter Thomas Moran gave the world one of the first views of the Grand Canyon. His work can be seen in museums all over the world. Other artists, including Maynard Dixon and Frederic Remington, painted colorful scenes of Arizona during the late 1800s and early 1900s.

Arizona's American Indians are known for their pottery, woven baskets, and blankets. Navajo blankets and rugs of every imaginable color are prized throughout the world. American Indian silversmiths have also gained recognition as creators of ornate jewelry.

Celebrated novelist Zane Grey captured the history and beauty of Arizona in his writing. Although born in Ohio, Grey spent much of his time at an Arizona hunting lodge and told many tales of Western adventure set in the state. Another writer, Oliver La Farge, won the Pulitzer Prize in 1930 for *Laughing Boy*. The book, about a Navajo couple, was the first novel about American Indian life to win the prize.

Novelist Zane Grey wrote more than ninety books in his lifetime.

Steven Spielberg wrote and directed his first full-length film, Firelight, *when he was just 16 years old.*

Music lovers attend the concerts of the Phoenix Symphony. The Arizona Opera divides its performance dates between Tucson and Phoenix. Jazz is supported in Scottsdale by an organization called Jazz in Arizona, in Sedona by Jazz on the Rocks, and in Tucson by the Tucson Jazz Society. Innovative jazz musician and composer Charles Mingus was born in Nogales. Arizonans have made their mark in rock and pop music as well. Singers Stevie Nicks and Jordin Sparks were both born in Phoenix.

Director Steven Spielberg made his first movies while growing up in the Phoenix area. He went on to direct some of the most popular films in Hollywood history, such as *E.T.*, *Raiders of the Lost Ark*, and *Jurassic Park*.

Though author Stephenie Meyer set her Twilight Saga in the overcast city of Forks, Washington, she makes her home in sunny Phoenix.

Actress Emma Stone was a member of the Valley Youth Theater in Phoenix. She starred in her first play, *The Wind in the Willows*, at age 11.

Novelist Terry McMillan was a professor at the University of Arizona.

Sports

Arizona is full of options for outdoor activities. People can water-ski in the warm sun and then bundle up for snow skiing on Mount Lemmon or the Arizona Snowbowl. The state's rivers and lakes provide great fishing and boating opportunities. Because of the warm climate, Arizonans can bicycle, rock climb, swim, and jog throughout the year. In season, hunters can track antelope, black bear, buffalo, or javelina. Tennis, baseball, and hiking are other ways to spend time outdoors in Arizona.

Golf is a favorite year-round activity in Arizona. Many resorts and retirement communities are centered around golf courses. About 11 million rounds of golf are played every year on the state's 350 courses. Amateur golfers are not the only athletes to enjoy the stunning Arizona courses. The Professional Golfers' Association of America (PGA) and the Ladies Professional Golf Association (LPGA) often visit Arizona courses during their tours.

Danica Patrick, one of the best-known racecar drivers, makes her home in Scottsdale. In 2009 she placed third at the Indianapolis 500, the highest finish for any woman in history.

There is no shortage of professional sports teams to cheer for in Arizona. Football fans support the Arizona Cardinals, who play at the University of Phoenix Stadium in Glendale. During baseball season, fans can watch the Arizona Diamondbacks in Phoenix. Basketball fans root for the Phoenix Suns of the National Basketball Association and the Phoenix Mercury of the Women's National Basketball Association. In spite of the climate, Arizonans even have a professional ice hockey team to watch, the Phoenix Coyotes.

Arizona's warm weather lures 15 major league baseball teams to Arizona for spring training in the Cactus League.

Olympic gymnast Kerri Strug is from Tucson. She captured hearts when she competed in the 1996 Olympics despite a badly injured ankle, helping the U.S. team win its first gold medal ever.

Arizona's professional football team, the Cardinals, played in St. Louis before moving to Phoenix and in Chicago before that. The franchise dates back to 1920, the first year of the National Football League.

Arizona's first major league baseball team, the Arizona Diamondbacks, plays its home games at Chase Field in Phoenix. The team came to the state in 1998.

National Averages Comparison

T he United States is a federal republic, consisting of fifty states and the District of Columbia. Alaska and Hawai'i are the only non-contiguous, or non-touching, states in the nation. Today, the United States of America is the third-largest country in the world in population. The United States Census Bureau takes a census, or count of all the people, every ten years. It also regularly collects other kinds of data about the population and the economy. How does Arizona compare to the national average?

Comparison Chart

United States 2010 Census Data *	USA	Arizona
Admission to Union	NA	February 14, 1912
Land Area (in square miles)	3,537,438.44	113,634.57
Population Total	308,745,538	6,392,017
Population Density (people per square mile)	87.28	56.25
Population Percentage Change (April 1, 2000, to April 1, 2010)	9.7%	24.6%
White Persons (percent)	72.4%	73.0%
Black Persons (percent)	12.6%	4.1%
American Indian and Alaska Native Persons (percent)	0.9%	4.6%
Asian Persons (percent)	4.8%	2.8%
Native Hawaiian and Other Pacific Islander Persons (percent)	0.2%	0.2%
Some Other Race (percent)	6.2%	11.9%
Persons Reporting Two or More Races (percent)	2.9%	3.4%
Persons of Hispanic or Latino Origin (percent)	16.3%	29.6%
Not of Hispanic or Latino Origin (percent)	83.7%	70.4%
Median Household Income	$52,029	$51,009
Percentage of People Age 25 or Over Who Have Graduated from High School	80.4%	84.2%

*All figures are based on the 2010 United States Census, with the exception of the last two items.

How to Improve My Community

Strong communities make strong states. Think about what features are important in your community. What do you value? Education? Health? Forests? Safety? Beautiful spaces? Government works to help citizens create ideal living conditions that are fair to all by providing services in communities. Consider what changes you could make in your community. How would they improve your state as a whole? Using this concept web as a guide, write a report that outlines the features you think are most important in your community and what improvements could be made. A strong state needs strong communities.

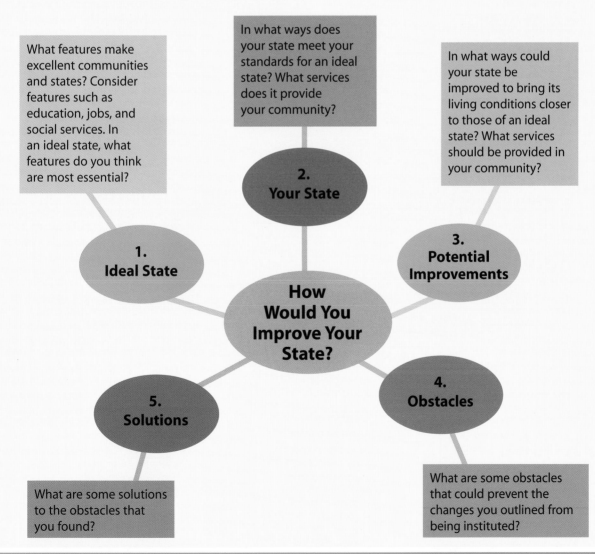

What features make excellent communities and states? Consider features such as education, jobs, and social services. In an ideal state, what features do you think are most essential?

In what ways does your state meet your standards for an ideal state? What services does it provide your community?

In what ways could your state be improved to bring its living conditions closer to those of an ideal state? What services should be provided in your community?

1. Ideal State

2. Your State

3. Potential Improvements

How Would You Improve Your State?

5. Solutions

4. Obstacles

What are some solutions to the obstacles that you found?

What are some obstacles that could prevent the changes you outlined from being instituted?

Exercise Your Mind!

Think about these questions and then use your research skills to find the answers and learn more fascinating facts about Arizona. A teacher, librarian, or parent may be able to help you locate the best sources to use in your research.

5 True or False? Agave is an American Indian group in Arizona.

1 True or False? There used to be volcanoes in Arizona.

6 What kind of fine cotton is named for one of Arizona's American Indian peoples?

2 What made the Apaches such great warriors?

7 Frank Lloyd Wright spent his winters in Scottsdale and died in Phoenix in 1959. What did he do that made him famous?

3 What Arizona senator was the Republican candidate for president in 2008?

4 What are Gila, Pinaleño, Huachuca, Santa Catalina, and Superstition?

8 True or False? London Bridge now carries Interstate 40 over Lake Havasu to California.

Words to Know

adobe: sun-dried brick

ancestry: distant relatives

bilingual: a person who is able to use two languages, especially with equal ability

buttes: tall columns of rock

capitol: a building occupied by a state legislature

dude ranches: resorts that offer activities typical of a ranch

expedition: a journey of exploration

gorge: narrow, steep-sided valley

hydroelectricity: water-generated power

irrigation: supplying land with water by using streams, canals, dams, and other methods

isolated: set apart or away from human contact

lariat: a rope used to tether a horse

mariachi: Mexican band

mesas: flat-topped hills with clifflike sides

petrified: stonelike

treaty: formal agreement between two parties

Index

Log on to www.av2books.com

AV² by Weigl brings you media enhanced books that support active learning. Go to www.av2books.com, and enter the special code found on page 2 of this book. You will gain access to enriched and enhanced content that supplements and complements this book. Content includes video, audio, web links, quizzes, a slide show, and activities.

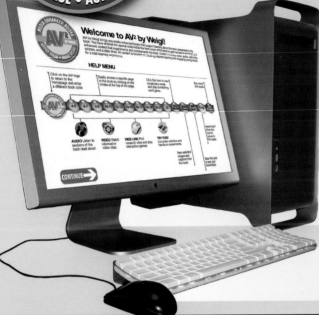

Audio
Listen to sections of the book read aloud.

Video
Watch informative video clips.

Embedded Weblinks
Gain additional information for research.

Try This!
Complete activities and hands-on experiments.

WHAT'S ONLINE?

Try This!	Embedded Weblinks	Video	EXTRA FEATURES
Test your knowledge of the state in a mapping activity.	Discover more attractions in Arizona.	Watch a video introduction to Arizona.	**Audio** Listen to sections of the book read aloud.
Find out more about precipitation in your city.	Learn more about the history of the state.	Watch a video about the features of the state.	**Key Words** Study vocabulary, and complete a matching word activity.
Plan what attractions you would like to visit in the state.	Learn the full lyrics of the state song.		**Slide Show** View images and captions, and prepare a presentation.
Learn more about the early natural resources of the state.			
Write a biography about a notable resident of Arizona.			**Quizzes** Test your knowledge.
Complete an educational census activity.			

AV² was built to bridge the gap between print and digital. We encourage you to tell us what you like and what you want to see in the future.

Sign up to be an AV² Ambassador at www.av2books.com/ambassador.